BRILLIANT WOMEN

PIONEERS OF SCIENCE AND TECHNOLOGY

Written by Georgia Amson-Bradshaw
Illustrated by Rita Petruccioli

BARRON'S

CONTENTS

PIONEERS OF SCIENCE AND TECHNOLOGY

HERE'S A QUICK RIDDLE FOR YOU TO TRY OUT ON YOUR FRIENDS.

A boy and his dad go to watch a football game. As they are driving home, their car is involved in an accident. The boy is rushed to the hospital in an ambulance, where a surgeon is ready and waiting to treat him. But when he arrives, the surgeon says, "Oh no! This boy is my son!" How can this be?

If you are feeling a bit baffled by this riddle, you're not alone. Most people can't think of the right answer. If you guessed correctly that the surgeon is the boy's mother, give yourself a big pat on the back!

Even in today's modern world, not everyone automatically imagines women working in science and technology professions, such as being a surgeon, an engineer, a physicist, or a mathematician. But, as the brilliantly brainy women in this book show, women have been working—and excelling—in science and technology for a very long time.

Some of the names you might already know. Double Nobel Prize-winning scientist, Marie Curie, and mathematician, Ada Lovelace, are famous figures from history. But you'll also get to meet some of the brilliant women who are pushing boundaries and solving problems today—from leprosy specialist Indira Nath to technology entrepreneur Juliana Rotich.

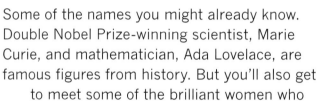

If you are a science-mad whiz kid, take a look at **pages 44–45** to find out how YOU can get involved in science. Who knows? You might be the next science and technology genius to go down in history!

CAROLINE HERSCHEL

Starting out as her brother's assistant, Caroline later became the first woman to earn a salary for the scientific study of the night sky.

ASTRONOMER

Caroline Herschel was a scientific expert on celestial bodies, such as stars, moons, comets, and nebulae.

LIVED: March 16, 1750–January 9, 1848

BORN IN: Hanover (Germany)

WORKED IN: Hanover (Germany) and Bath (UK)

Caroline was born in Germany, the eighth child in her family. Being a child wasn't a lot of fun for Caroline, because her mother didn't want her to study and instead made her do most of the housework. When Caroline was ten years old she caught the deadly disease typhus. She survived, but because of the illness she never grew taller than 4 ft 3 in (1 m 33 cm). Because of this, her family assumed she would never marry, and thought it was better she learned to be a house servant than get an education.

Oh look, a star... Oh look, another star...

Caroline's dad was a musician. She loved music too, and learned to sing accompanied by her brother, William, who played the violin, harpsichord, and the oboe. When her dad died, Caroline moved to England where William was living. In England, William began working as an astronomer, and Caroline's career in astronomy also took off when she started working as his assistant.

At first William put her to work polishing the mirrors for his telescopes. Later he got her to help him by scanning the skies every night to catalog the stars. It was a slow, repetitive task, and one she didn't enjoy much in the beginning.

After a while Caroline began to really enjoy astronomy, and during her stargazing she discovered several comets and nebulae. William became the official astronomer for King George III, and as William's assistant the King started to pay Caroline a salary of £50 per year for her work. That is the equivalent of $7,980 (£5,700, at a rate of exchange of £1.00 = $1.40) in today's money, a considerable sum in those days. This made her the first woman to be paid for astronomy at a time when most men were not paid for their scientific work.

Along with her brother, Caroline discovered more than 2,400 astronomical objects such as stars, comets, and asteroids. Her patient, thorough astronomical work contributed a lot to our knowledge of the skies. In particular, she discovered eight comets, once riding all through the night to register her findings at the Royal Observatory in Greenwich before anyone else could!

In 1828, she was awarded the Gold Medal of the Royal Astronomical Society, something a woman was not awarded again until 1996—168 years later! Along with Mary Somerville, who was another prominent woman scientist of the era (see page 38), Caroline was elected as an honorary member of the Royal Astronomical Society. The two of them were the first women members.

STARGAZE LIKE CAROLINE

The best way to see stars is to get away from any streetlights, floodlights, and house lights. What better excuse to get your family and friends together and go on a countryside camping trip to look at the night sky? Bundle up warm, bring marshmallows for toasting and, once it gets dark, see what constellations you can spot.

There are apps that can be downloaded for smartphones that will help you identify constellations and individual stars in the sky. If you have a telescope, see if you can spot the patterns of craters on the Moon that have been formed by asteroids hitting its surface. One of the Moon's craters is called C. Herschel, after Caroline herself.

Even if you can't travel very far, it's still worth stargazing from your garden or local park. For regular stargazing practice, search online for astronomy clubs in your local area.

MARY ANNING

Born in poverty, Mary began fossil-hunting to earn money.
Her discoveries changed our thinking about
how life developed on Earth.

PALEONTOLOGIST

Mary Anning collected and studied fossils
of ancient creatures, advancing our
understanding of prehistoric life.

LIVED:	May 21, 1799–March 9, 1847
BORN IN:	Lyme Regis (UK)
WORKED IN:	Lyme Regis (UK)

Mary Anning's family was very poor. She and her brother Joseph were the only two of ten siblings who survived childhood, though as a baby Mary had a lucky escape when she was being looked after by a neighbor. Three women and baby Mary were underneath a tree when it was struck by lightning! The three women were instantly killed, and only baby Mary miraculously survived. As she grew up, people in her village said the lightning strike was the cause of her intelligence and curiosity.

To help her family earn money, Mary collected fossils along the Dorset coast, which they sold to collectors and geologists. She searched bravely and tirelessly, especially in winter when storms exposed more fossils. The unstable cliffs were dangerous and she was once nearly killed in a landslide.

The geologists wrote about the fossils, but Mary herself was not included in the exclusive, scientific community—despite the importance of her findings. In 1811, Mary discovered the skeleton of the prehistoric sea creature, the ichthyosaur. The finding caused a sensation, because it began to make scientists question the history of the Earth, at a time when most people believed that God had created the planet 6,000 years ago. But despite the buzz about the skeleton, the scientific papers written about it never mentioned Mary's name.

As well as the ichthyosaur, Mary also discovered plesiosaurs and pterosaurs. She even solved a scientific puzzle that none of the other experts could crack: she figured out that stones, called "coprolites," found in the intestine area of the skeletons, were fossilized dinosaur poo!

What on Earth could it be?

How shall I tell him he's holding a poo?

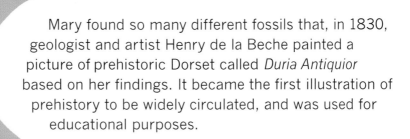

Mary found so many different fossils that, in 1830, geologist and artist Henry de la Beche painted a picture of prehistoric Dorset called *Duria Antiquior* based on her findings. It became the first illustration of prehistory to be widely circulated, and was used for educational purposes.

Mary's poor background and the fact she was a woman meant that she received very little recognition for her work during her lifetime. After her death her friend and president of the Geological Society, Henry de la Beche, published a eulogy for her. The famous writer Charles Dickens also wrote an article about Mary, and she may have inspired the famous tongue-twister, "She sells seashells on the seashore." In recent times, due to her expertise in finding fossils, she has come to be recognized as one of the most important British women in science.

DISCOVER PREHISTORY LIKE MARY

The painting *Duria Antiquior* shows an "action shot" of the fossilized animals that had been discovered by Mary along the Dorset coast. Henry de la Beche sold prints of his painting to raise money for Mary. In the image, an ichthyosaur is biting the neck of a plesiosaur, and the plesiosaur is even shown making the droppings that will become coprolite.

The split-level view reveals the scene both above and below the surface of the water. Research what dinosaurs and prehistoric creatures lived in your area, and create your own "action shot" in the style of the *Duria Antiquior*.

ADA LOVELACE

Creative and brilliant, Ada Lovelace developed the first "computer program" nearly a hundred years before the first computers were actually built.

COMPUTER PROGRAMMER AND MATHEMATICIAN

Ada Lovelace was an expert at math, and she theorized how a machine could be used to calculate more than just numbers.

LIVED: December 10, 1815–November 27, 1852

BORN IN: London (UK)

WORKED IN: London (UK)

Hello Ada!

Augusta Ada Byron was the daughter of the famous poet Lord Byron and the English aristocrat Lady Anne Isabella Byron. It was her dad who chose the name, Ada, that she was known by, but when baby Ada was only one month old her parents separated. Her mom did not trust Lord Byron because of his reckless behavior, always spending all his money and breaking his promises!

Anne Isabella thought that Lord Byron's rash behavior and poetic imagination was a kind of "madness" and she was worried Ada would take after her dad. When Ada told her mother of her idea to build a steam-powered flying horse, Lady Byron became even more concerned! She wanted Ada to be sensible, so she insisted Ada be taught math and science from a young age. This was a very unusual education for girls at the time, but Ada was very clever and excelled at her studies.

Hmm, you're actually quite clever for a girl.

No kidding, old man.

When she was 17, she met the mechanical engineer and mathematician Charles Babbage at a party. Charles Babbage had no time for people he thought were foolish or stupid, and he often became very angry when other people made mistakes. But even though Ada was a young woman, her mathematical talent was so great they became good friends.

Charles Babbage came up with the idea of a mechanical computer that could complete mathematical calculations, which he called his Analytical Engine. Instructions could be fed into the machine using hole-punched cards. The Analytical Engine really captured Ada's imagination. She worked with Charles, translating some writings about the machine, to which she added many pages of her own notes about how the machine could be used.

Using very complex math, Ada explained how the machine could be "programmed" to do all sorts of calculations. Even though the machine hadn't actually been built, and modern computers would not be invented for over a hundred years, Ada had written the first ever computer program!

Thanks to her powerful imagination and intelligence, Ada was also able to think about possible future tasks that computers would be able to complete beyond simply calculating numbers. She suggested they could do things such as compose music, or be useful to science—which has come true.

Ada knew that her visionary qualities were unique. She said, "I believe myself to possess a most singular combination of qualities exactly fitted to make me pre-eminently a discoverer of the hidden realities of nature."

PROGRAM COMPUTERS LIKE ADA

Nowadays computers are in every area of our lives and do all sorts of things, just like Ada predicted. In fact, you can write a program to make music with your computer, just as she imagined! Visit the website scratch.mit.edu. To program a musical track, click on the "create" tab at the top of the page. Next, click on the link on the right-hand side of the page for the step-by-step tutorial called "Make Music." This will take you through steps to program your own musical melody and animation.

MARIE CURIE

This double Nobel Prize-winning woman made history several times over, discovering radioactivity and new chemical elements.

PHYSICIST AND CHEMIST

Marie Curie's study of radioactivity advanced our scientific understanding in physics (the study of matter and energy) and chemistry (the study of substances).

LIVED: November 7, 1867–July 4, 1934

BORN IN: Warsaw (Poland)

WORKED IN: Paris (France)

When she was a young girl, Marie's dad taught her and her brothers and sisters at home. He was a math and physics teacher, and he brought home laboratory equipment from the school he taught at. Marie loved science and wanted to go on and study at a university, but in Poland at that time it was forbidden for women to enter higher education.

She attended an illegal underground school called the "Flying University" that taught women students in secret. The classes would regularly change locations around the city, in order to avoid the teachers and students from being arrested! However, Marie knew that to get a proper education she would have to go to an official university. She saved up for several years until she had enough money to go to the famous university, the Sorbonne, in Paris, France.

Marie completed two degrees in Paris, one in physics and one in math. She also met and fell in love with a young professor named Pierre Curie. They worked together studying the mysterious "X-rays" that some materials give off. Marie described these materials as "radioactive." She was the first person to use this word, and through her experiments she discovered two new elements. They were called radium and polonium (after her homeland, Poland).

In 1906, Pierre was killed in an accident. Marie was devastated, but was determined to honor his memory. She continued her work and took over his role as professor at the Sorbonne, becoming the first woman to teach there. Experiments with radium showed Marie that it could be used to kill cancerous cells.

At the beginning of the 20th century, this new material radium really fired people's imaginations and was believed to have all sorts of wonderful, magical healing properties. It was put in lots of products, from chocolate to children's toys! People did not know at that time how dangerous radioactive materials were.

RADIOACTIVE CHOCOLATE KIDS' FAVORITE!

Marie won two Nobel Prizes for her work, one in 1903 and one in 1911. She was the first woman to be awarded the prestigious award, and she was also the first (and so far, only) woman to win twice. She is now one of the most famous scientists in history.

EXPERIMENT LIKE MARIE

X-rays are far too dangerous to experiment with at home, however, you can do an experiment to see the effect of a different type of radiation. X-rays are a type of light—but one that we can't see with our eyes. Ultraviolet, or UV light, is another type of light that we can't see with our eyes, but we can see its effects. Along with visible light, they are both given off by the Sun.

To see the effects of UV rays, place a piece of colored paper in a sunny spot with a cardboard cut-out shape in the center. Leave it for a few days, then remove the cardboard shape. You should see a dark outline where the paper has been protected from the UV rays.

LISE MEITNER

Facing discrimination for being a woman, then in danger for being Jewish,
Lise Meitner tirelessly battled many obstacles to pursue her passion for physics.

NUCLEAR PHYSICIST

Lise Meitner studied atoms, the
tiny building blocks of all stuff, and
the energy that can be released
when they are split
even smaller.

LIVED: November 7, 1878–October 27, 1968

BORN IN: Vienna (Austria)

WORKED IN: Berlin (Germany) and Stockholm (Sweden)

> *How? What? Why?*

ise's family lived in Vienna, Austria. They were a well-off Jewish family, and Lise was one of eight children. She was a very curious child, full of questions. A natural scientist, by the age of eight she was studying things about the world around her, such as how light splits into colors on oil slicks. She kept a notebook of her scientific observations under her pillow.

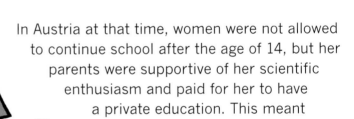

In Austria at that time, women were not allowed to continue school after the age of 14, but her parents were supportive of her scientific enthusiasm and paid for her to have a private education. This meant Lise was able to study at the University of Vienna, and later the University of Berlin. When World War I broke out in 1914, Lise helped wounded soldiers by taking X-rays of their injuries.

In Berlin, Lise met a chemist named Otto Hahn, and together they worked on particles and radioactivity. She enjoyed her work very much, but when the National Socialists (Nazis) rose to power in the 1930s the situation became very dangerous for Lise, who had Jewish heritage.

The Nazis passed a law banning scientists from leaving the country, and it became clear that Lise would have to escape Germany secretly. Her colleagues helped with her escape preparations, and Otto Hahn gave her his mother's diamond ring in case she needed it to bribe Nazi guards.

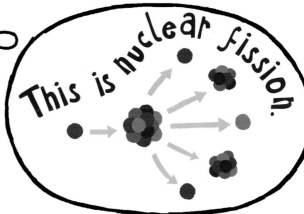

This is nuclear fission.

Lise escaped to Sweden, and stayed in contact with Otto via post. In Sweden, she realized that it would be possible to split an atom into smaller particles, releasing lots of energy. This is nuclear fission, the basis of nuclear power, and the nuclear bomb.

Lise was very disapproving of the use of nuclear technology in weapons-making, and she refused a job offer from the USA to work on nuclear weapons, saying, "I will have nothing to do with a bomb!" She faced great danger and was disadvantaged throughout much of her life due to prejudice she faced as both a woman and a Jew, but she never gave up. She said, "Life need not be easy, provided only that it is not empty."

EXPLORE LIKE LISE

It's not very safe or practical to try and recreate nuclear experiments in your bedroom! But that doesn't mean you can't explore like Lise. Being a professional scientist starts with observing the world around you, just like Lise did with her notebook when she was a young girl.

Get a notebook and go outside. Look at the world around you and try to really notice small details and patterns in the way things are. Look at how things move, for example, watch how spilled water runs and collects on a pavement. Look at plants through a magnifying lens. Touch different materials to see how warm or cold they feel. Record your observations in your notebook, and try to figure out ideas as to why things are the way they are. This is how scientists come up with "hypotheses," or theories.

B

12.1 ft (3.7) m

A

C

smooth

rough

BARBARA McCLINTOCK

Barbara McClintock made many groundbreaking discoveries about genetics by studying corn plants.

CYTOGENETICIST

Barbara McClintock studied how genes can change the behavior of cells, affecting the appearance of plants, such as the color of corn kernels.

LIVED: June 16, 1902–September 2, 1992

BORN IN: Hartford, Connecticut (USA)

WORKED IN: Ithaca and Long Island, New York (USA)

When she was born, Barbara was given the name Eleanor McClintock, but as a young girl her parents noticed a strong independent streak in her. They decided to change Eleanor's name to Barbara, because they thought it was better suited to her strong personality. At school Barbara discovered a love for science, and told her parents she wanted to go to a university to study. Her mom worried that no man would want a scientist for a wife! But Barbara didn't care one bit about that. She was determined to pursue her passion. Her dad, who was a doctor, supported her and in 1919, she went to Cornell University to study biology.

At Cornell, Barbara began to work on the subject that would occupy most of her career, studying the genetics of corn plants (which are also called "maize"). She was fascinated by how some purple kinds of corn had kernels of different colors: some that were purple, some that were white, and some that were speckled.

Barbara's work centered around the study of chromosomes, which are tiny structures that all living things have inside their cells. These structures contain genes, which are like microscopic instructions in our bodies that control things, such as how we look (for example, whether we have blue or brown eyes). Barbara wanted to figure out how these genes affected the appearance of the corn.

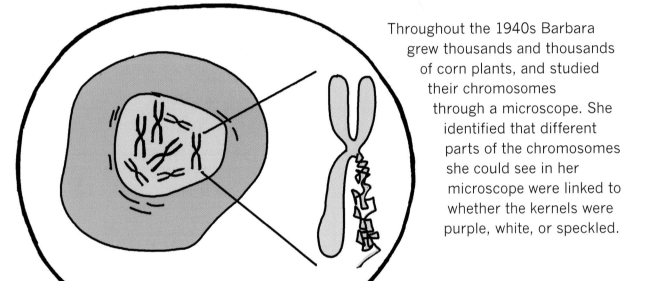

Throughout the 1940s Barbara grew thousands and thousands of corn plants, and studied their chromosomes through a microscope. She identified that different parts of the chromosomes she could see in her microscope were linked to whether the kernels were purple, white, or speckled.

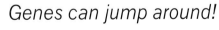

Genes can jump around!

Barbara also realized how sometimes bits of those genetic instructions would get "swapped around" when cells reproduce. This explains how a purple corn cell could reproduce but make a white corn cell instead. This was her famous "jumping gene" discovery.

Barbara liked to work alone and her research was way ahead of its time. As a result, her research was largely ignored by fellow scientists. It was only in the 1960s and 1970s that people began to understand the importance of her findings, and she was finally recognized with the Nobel Prize in Physiology or Medicine in 1983, for her contribution to the understanding of genetics.

Often, the Nobel Prize is awarded to teams of people, however, Barbara's prize was awarded to her alone, the first Nobel Prize of this type to go to an individual woman.

OBSERVE LIKE BARBARA

You are probably familiar with the yellow sweetcorn that we eat, but why not try growing some of the purple corn that led to Barbara making her amazing discoveries? You can observe the different colors in the kernels up close, and compare the cobs of different plants to see how the patterns change. To find seeds for purple corn (also called "Indian corn") search online, and follow the planting instructions on the seed packet.

KATHERINE JOHNSON

An incredibly talented mathematician, Katherine Johnson was one of the "human computers" that helped put U.S. astronauts into space.

ANALYTIC GEOMETRY

Katherine Johnson was an all-round talented mathematician, but her knowledge of analytic geometry (a type of math that uses coordinates) was essential to her work at NASA.

BORN: August 26, 1918

BORN IN: White Sulphur Springs, West Virginia (USA)

WORKED IN: Hampton, Virginia (USA)

29

As a little girl, Katherine loved numbers. She counted everything—from the steps she took to reach the church, to the knives and forks when she washed the dishes. Her mathematical talent was so obvious from such an early age that she started high school four years early at just ten years old, and went to college at age 14!

In many states in the USA at that time, there were laws enforcing "segregation," which meant black students were not allowed to go to the same schools and universities as white students. Getting a good education wasn't straightforward for Katherine, because the county her family lived in did not have any universities for black students. This meant she had to attend a university over 124 mi (200 km) away.

In 1952, she heard that NACA (the organization that later became NASA) was hiring mathematicians. In those days, complex mathematical calculations were carried out mainly by humans, not machines. People who did the calculations were called "computers" so Katherine became one of the "computers in skirts" at NACA, the all-women team of mathematicians who did the number-crunching for the research team.

In keeping with the state laws, the workplace at NACA was segregated. This meant white women and black women worked separately, even having to use separate toilets and drinking fountains. When NACA became NASA in 1958 the workplace was desegregated, but there were still barriers against her as a woman. For a long time Katherine was not allowed to put her name as the author of research reports, and instead had to use the name of a male colleague.

Putting a man in space for the first time meant figuring out incredibly complex mathematics, and Katherine did a lot of the calculations for the USA's first ever human spaceflight, in 1961. She was so good at her work that, the following year, astronaut John Glenn specifically requested that Katherine check the calculations for his flight orbiting Earth, rather than rely on the calculations from the machines. John Glenn's flight was a success, and it marked a turning point in the Space Race between the USA and Russia as to who could put a man on the Moon first.

Get Katherine to do the math!

Katherine was employed at NASA for over 30 years, and during that time she worked extremely hard to overcome the barriers that were put in front of her as a black woman. As well as pushing to have her own name on research reports, she fought to attend high-level meetings, where previously women had not been welcome. In 2015, President Obama honored Katherine with the Presidential Medal of Freedom, the highest honor a civilian can receive in the USA.

SOLVE PROBLEMS LIKE KATHERINE

Reckon you've got what it takes to solve math problems about space? Flex your math muscles on the NASA "Space Math" website: spacemath.gsfc.nasa.gov/grade35.html. Try the math problems to test your skills on the sorts of topics that Katherine herself worked on! Figure out how the orbit of the International Space Station changes, or use geometry—the same type of math that Katherine excelled at—to calculate when planets will line up.

JANE GOODALL

A fearless explorer with big dreams, Jane Goodall made amazing scientific discoveries about chimpanzees by studying them in the wild.

PRIMATOLOGIST

Jane Goodall is an expert on primates, the group of animals that includes monkeys, chimpanzees, gorillas, and humans.

BORN: April 3, 1934

BORN IN: London (UK)

WORKED IN: Gombe (Tanzania) and Cambridge (UK)

Jane!

Jane Goodall was always fascinated by animals. Visiting a farm when she was just four years old, she hid in a hen house for hours to discover how chickens laid eggs. She didn't realize her poor mom was rushing around outside looking for her, absolutely worried sick!

When she was ten years old Jane read the book *Tarzan of the Apes*. It was about a man raised by apes, and his wife—who was also called Jane! That's when she knew that her dream was to move to Africa, live in the wild, and write books about the animals there.

Jane's family didn't have a lot of money. Moving to Africa to study animals seemed like an impossible dream. But Jane worked hard as a waitress, saved up, and in 1957 at the age of 23, she took a boat to Kenya.

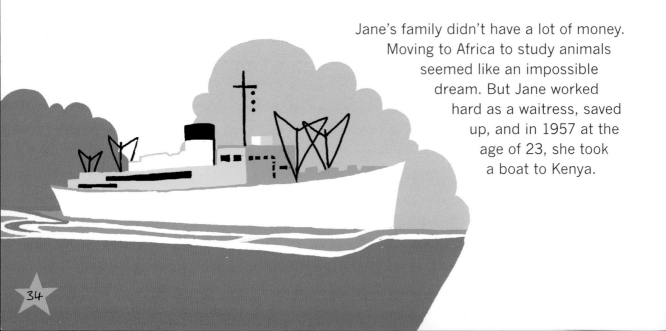

She soon got an opportunity to start studying the chimpanzees that lived in the jungle in Tanzania. At first the chimpanzees were frightened and ran away from her. Slowly, they got used to her presence, and allowed her to watch them close up.

Don't look now, she's back!

While observing the chimpanzees, Jane discovered something amazing. The chimpanzees were making simple tools for catching termites, by stripping the leaves off twigs, and poking them into termite mounds. Until that time, it was believed that humans were the only creatures to make and use tools. When she told her mentor, Louis Leakey, he said, "Now we must redefine man, redefine tools, or accept chimpanzees as humans." This was a major scientific discovery!

We must respect animals like we respect other people.

Louis Leakey told Jane she needed to get a degree to get funding for her scientific work. She went to Cambridge University to study ethology—the study of animal behavior—and became only the eighth person to be allowed to gain a Ph.D. without having a degree.

In the beginning Jane got a rather frosty welcome at Cambridge. Many of the academics there accused her of being unscientific in her work, because she had given the chimpanzees names instead of numbers, and she had committed what in their eyes was a terrible sin—believing that the chimpanzees were feeling emotions, seeming happy or sad. The idea that chimpanzees can feel emotions is much less controversial now, but at the time, as a young, self-educated woman, Jane had to fight hard to have her research taken seriously.

Jane worked with chimpanzees in Africa for many more years, and made several other important discoveries. In 1977, she founded the Jane Goodall Institute, a global wildlife and environment conservation organization. She also founded Roots & Shoots, which helps young people get involved in environmental and wildlife conservation in their own local area.

CAMPAIGN LIKE JANE

Do you love animals and want to help protect the environment? Start a nature club with your friends. Study the plants and animals around where you live, and come up with ways to improve your local area for the resident insects and animals.

MORE SCIENCE AND TECHNOLOGY GENIUSES

The list of brilliant women in science and technology doesn't stop there! Here are even more groundbreaking women scientists that you should know about, from the present day right back to the ancient Greek period.

HYPATIA

LIVED: c. CE 355–415

BORN IN: Alexandria (Egypt)

WORKED IN: Egypt

Ancient Greek mathematician, philosopher, and astronomer Hypatia was one of the earliest recorded female mathematicians. She was taught by her father, Theon, who was a well-respected scholar.

Hypatia was educated in Athens in mainland Greece, but as an adult lived in the city of Alexandria in ancient Egypt, which was part of the Eastern Roman Empire and had a famous library. She eventually surpassed her father's knowledge, and became the head of the Neoplatonist School in Alexandria, teaching the works of Plato and Aristotle to students who came from miles around. Hypatia was killed by rioting Christians, due to the religious unrest in the city.

MARY SOMERVILLE

LIVED: December 26, 1780–November 29, 1872

BORN IN: Jedburgh (Scotland)

WORKED IN: Scotland and England

As a child Mary was not given much education. Following her family's wishes, she married her cousin, a Russian navy captain who also did not approve of her studying. After he died just three years later, Mary was free to dedicate herself to her love of math and astronomy. Her second husband, who she married in 1812, was proud and supportive of his wife's self-taught knowledge. They moved to London, and Mary became friends with scientists such as Charles Babbage and Caroline Herschel.

Mary wrote many books on different scientific topics, including a book called *Physical Geography* which was used as a textbook until the early 20th century. She became a well-respected figure, being accepted into the Royal Astronomical Society alongside Caroline Hershel, the first women to be members of the respected scientific society.

RACHEL CARSON

LIVED: May 27, 1907–April 14, 1964

BORN IN: Springdale, Pennsylvania (USA)

WORKED IN: USA

Rachel grew up on a large farm, where she learned about nature and animals. The ocean was a particular topic of interest for her, and she ended up studying biology, and later specializing in marine biology when she went to Pennsylvania College for Women (now Chatham University), then received an M.A. in zoology from Johns Hopkins University. After graduating she got a job writing environmental literature for the U.S. Bureau of Fisheries. Rachel wrote several books about the ocean and the environment. Her most famous book, *Silent Spring*, is about the harmful effects of pesticides on the natural world. She became very involved in nature conservation, and she testified before Congress about the dangers of pesticides.

DOROTHY HODGKIN

LIVED: May 12, 1910–July 29, 1994

BORN IN: Cairo (Egypt)

WORKED IN: UK

Dorothy's father was an archaeologist, and she was born in Cairo, in Egypt. She spent much of her childhood traveling around different places in the Middle East. She did well at school, and then went to Oxford University to study chemistry. She received her Ph.D. from Cambridge University. After graduating, she worked at both Universities. Her work was on protein crystallography, which is a technique that uses X-rays to look at the atoms of proteins. Dorothy found crystallography absolutely fascinating, and through her dedication to the work she identified the structure of penicillin, insulin, and the vitamin B12. She became the third woman to win the Nobel Prize in Chemistry.

CHIEN-SHIUNG WU

LIVED: May 31, 1912–February 16, 1997
BORN IN: Liuhe, Taicang (China)
WORKED IN: USA

Chien-Shiung Wu was born near Shanghai in China. Her parents were strongly in favor of her having a good education, and they encouraged Wu to study hard. She studied physics at a University in China, but at her academic advisor's suggestion she left China in 1936 to continue her studies in the USA.

She became an expert in nuclear physics, and was recruited to the Manhattan Project—a team that developed nuclear weapons. After World War II she became a professor again, and made further breakthroughs in nuclear physics, for which she was awarded a Nobel Prize, as well as being given the nickname "the Queen of Nuclear Research."

ROSALIND FRANKLIN

LIVED: July 25, 1920–April 16, 1958
BORN IN: London (UK)
WORKED IN: UK

Rosalind Franklin was born into a well-off Jewish family in London. Her parents helped settle Jewish refugees from Europe who had escaped the Nazis, and her mother was involved in the struggle for voting rights for women. Rosalind was a very talented student, and went on to study chemistry at Cambridge University. She became an expert on X-ray images of substances, and in 1950 she started working on making X-ray images of DNA. This work led to the discovery of the structure of DNA. Rosalind died in 1958 at age 37 from ovarian cancer, but her colleagues on the same project were awarded a Nobel Prize in 1962 for their work.

INDIRA NATH

BORN: January 14, 1938
BORN IN: Andhra Pradesh (India)
WORKS IN: India

Indira knew when she was ten years old that she would become a doctor. When she was old enough to go to a university, Indira traveled to the UK to study for her medical degree, but she was committed to returning to India after graduating so she could use her skills and knowledge to the benefit of her home country.

India has the highest rates of leprosy in the world, and Indira was determined to make a breakthrough in the treatment and prevention of the disease. Indira identified a problem with sufferers' immune systems, which was a big step forward in developing treatments and vaccines. Thanks in large part to her research, the number of people in India suffering from leprosy has dropped from 4.5 million people, to fewer than 1 million today, and better treatments mean that the worst disfigurements from leprosy are now rare.

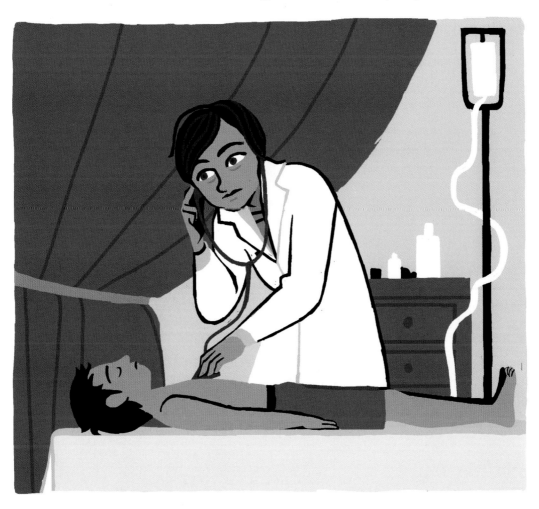

WANDA DÍAZ-MERCED

BORN: February 7, 1974

BORN IN: Gurabo (Puerto Rico)

WORKS IN: Puerto Rico, South Africa, and UK

As young girls growing up in Puerto Rico, Wanda and her sister used to dream of visiting distant galaxies in a space shuttle. Her family was poor, but Wanda's hard work led to her winning places on several science summer programs. She went on to study physics at the University of Puerto Rico, but tragedy struck when she lost her sight through illness. She later received a doctorate from the University of Glasgow and was a post-doctoral fellow at the South African Astronomical Observatory in Cape Town.

Wanda thought she wouldn't be able to continue with astrophysics, but rather than letting her disability prevent her from continuing in the field she loved, Wanda came up with a solution. Instead of relying on visual graphs of data, she translated the data into sound. She has since made scientific breakthroughs, finding patterns that would not have been noticed using visual methods alone.

JULIANA ROTICH

BORN: 1977

BORN IN: Kenya

WORKS IN: Kenya

Always passionate about technology, Juliana was the chair of her school computer club. She studied computer science at the University of Missouri in the U.S. and worked in the computer industry after she graduated. Then, in Kenya in 2008, violence broke out after the elections. During the confusion, Juliana realized how difficult it was to get accurate, up-to-date information about what was happening. She created Ushahidi, a website and communication platform that could be used by anyone to report and map incidents. The same technology is now used in many countries in various situations, for example, after natural disasters like earthquakes, or during conflicts, as well as for ongoing issues such as pollution. She also developed the BRCK, a self-powered portable WiFi router to ensure good Internet access in places without an Internet connection.

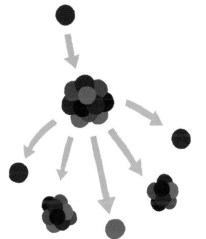

COUNTLESS OTHERS...

There are so many more incredible women making amazing discoveries and important contributions to science, technology, and math that there isn't space for on these pages. At this very moment, all around the world, some of the most cutting-edge science in the fields of robotics, materials science, medicine, environmental science, and anything else you can think of is being done by women. Who knows what astonishing scientific breakthroughs women will make next?

GET INVOLVED IN SCIENCE AND TECHNOLOGY!

There are hundreds of fun ways to pursue your passion for science and technology. Here are just a few suggestions to get you started.

GET INVOLVED IN CITIZEN SCIENCE!

Citizen science is a practical way to help out with actual, cutting-edge scientific research. Scientists often need tons of data to test and prove their theories, and sometimes this data can be very time-consuming or expensive to collect. Enter citizen science. In citizen science projects, normal people can go out and make observations, or take part in quizzes and activities online, which all go toward a scientist's REAL research project.

Citizen science projects range from things such as the RSPB's Big Garden Birdwatch, which asks people to record what bird species they spot in their gardens on specific days of the year, to online projects about all sorts of subjects. Search online for "citizen science" to see what you can find.

FIND A SCIENCE CLUB, OR START ONE YOURSELF

You can use the Internet or ask at a local library to see if there are any science clubs in your area. If there aren't, don't be put off—just start one yourself! Find some friends who are also interested in science, and ask a teacher or parent to help you organize space and resources. What sort of activities would you like to do in your club? If you want to do hands-on experiments you can find ideas for science projects and fun activities online, or in your local library. You might want to try new activities each week, or you might want to work on one big project— and even enter it into a competition.

ENTER A YOUNG PERSON'S SCIENCE COMPETITION

There are lots of national science competitions you can enter, either in teams or individually. If you need to put a team together or you need access to equipment, it's worth talking to your school to see if they can help.

GO TO A SCIENCE FESTIVAL

Science festivals can be an awesome way to witness some super cool fizzing and whizzing science. Events range from explanatory talks and expert-led demonstrations, to fun hands-on workshops where you get to test out the scientific principles for yourself! Look online to find out if any festivals are coming to a town near you.

LEARN TO CODE

If computers and digital technology are what really get you excited, look out for code clubs in your local area that can teach you how to write computer programs. Some volunteer-led organizations also run digital technology summer camps, where you can explore robotics, game development, and other cool skills.

GLOSSARY

Aristocrat Someone whose family has a high social rank, especially someone who has a title, such as Duke or Baroness.

Asteroid A chunk of rock traveling through space.

Astronomy The study of the Sun, Moon, planets, stars, and other objects in space.

Astrophysics The study of the physical and chemical structure of the stars, planets, and other objects in space.

Atom One of the tiny building blocks that make up all stuff.

Cells Small building blocks that make up living things.

Chromosome Structures in a living being's cells that contain genes.

Comet A chunk of dust and ice that travels through space.

Constellation A pattern of stars in the night sky.

Coprolite Fossilized dinosaur excrement.

DNA The acid in the cells of living things that carries genetic information.

Element A substance that is made up of only one type of atom.

Eulogy A speech or piece of writing praising a person who has died.

Fossil The shape or impression of a plant or animal that has been preserved in rock for a very long time.

Gene A microscopic "instruction" in a living thing's cells that determines what it will look like or how it will behave.

Geologist A scientist who studies rocks and fossils.

Geometry A branch of math that looks at shapes and angles, among other properties.

Hypothesis A scientific theory about why or how something happens.

Jew A person who believes in and practices the religion of Judaism. Jewish people were discriminated against by the Nazis in Europe in the 1920s and 1930s.

Leprosy An infectious disease that affects the skin and nerves.

Matter The scientific term for all stuff.

Nazi A member of the right-wing political party, led by Adolf Hitler, which was in power in Germany from 1933 to 1945.

Nebula (plural: nebulae) A cloud of dust and gas in space where new stars are formed.

Nuclear fission A scientific process where atoms, the tiny building blocks of all matter, are split into even tinier pieces releasing huge amounts of energy.

Orbit A curved path followed by a planet or an object as it moves around another object.

Pesticide A chemical that is used to kill insects that eat farmer's crops.

Ph.D. The abbreviation for doctor of philosophy, the highest college or university degree.

Radioactive A word that describes a substance that gives off certain types of rays that can't be seen with the naked eye.

Refugee A person who has been forced to leave their country, because there is a war or because of their political or religious beliefs.

FURTHER INFORMATION

WEBSITES

For a large selection of citizen science projects visit this platform for people-powered research. **www.zooniverse.org**

To find a student science fair in the United States, as well as over 70 other countries, regions, and territories, check out: **https://findafair.societyforscience.org/**

The Big Bang Competition is an annual science competition in the UK for young people. **www.thebigbangfair.co.uk**

Check out this comprehensive list of every science fair accessible through the World Wide Web, whether of global or local scope. **physics.usc.edu/ScienceFairs**

BOOKS

Women in Science: 50 Fearless Pioneers Who Changed the World by Rachel Ignotofsky (Wren & Rook, 2017)

Good Night Stories for Rebel Girls by Elena Favilli and Francesca Cavallo (Particular Books, 2017)

Fantastically Great Women Who Changed the World by Kate Pankhurst (Bloomsbury, 2016)

Scientists Who Made History series (Wayland, 2014)

Girls Think of Everything by Catherine Thimmesh (Houghton Mifflin, 2002)

INDEX

First edition for the United States, its territories and dependencies, the Philippine Republic, and Canada published in 2018 by Barron's Educational Series, Inc.

Text © copyright 2018 by Georgia Amson-Bradshaw
Illustrated by Rita Petruccioli
Volume © copyright 2018 by Hodder and Stoughton
First published in Great Britain in 2018 by Wayland, an imprint of Hachette Children's Group, part of Hodder & Stoughton

The right of Georgia Amson-Bradshaw to be identified as the author of this work has been asserted by her in accordance with the Copyright, Designs, and Patent Act of 1988.

All inquiries should be addressed to:
Barron's Educational Series, Inc.
250 Wireless Boulevard
Hauppauge, NY 11788
www.barronseduc.com

Library of Congress Control No: 2018939580

ISBN: 978-1-4380-1220-9

Date of Manufacture: May 2018
Manufactured by: WKT, Shenzhen, China

Printed in China
9 8 7 6 5 4 3 2 1

The website addresses (URLs) included in this book were valid at the time of going to press. However, it is possible that contents or addresses may have changed since the publication of this book. No responsibility for any such changes can be accepted by either the author or the publishers. The author and publishers recommend that all web searches be supervised by an adult.